UNEXPECTED GUESTS

By
Steven P. Schneider

BLUE LIGHT PRESS
1st WORLD
PUBLISHING

1ST WORLD LIBRARY
106 South Court Street
Fairfield, Iowa 52556
www.1stworldpublishing.com

BLUE LIGHT PRESS
PO Box 642, Fairfield, Iowa 52556

AUTHOR PHOTO
Rocky Lozano

BOOK DESIGN
Melanie Gendron
www.melaniegendron.com

COVER ART
"The Expectant Father"
Reefka Schneider
www.poetry-art.com

FIRST EDITION

LCCN: 2008931417

ISBN: 978-1-4218-9895-7

UNEXPECTED GUESTS

For
Reefka, Aaron, and Roni

ALSO BY STEVEN P. SCHNEIDER

Poetry:

Prairie Air Show (2000)

Literary Criticism:

Complexities of Motion: New Essays on A.R. Ammons's Long Poems (1999)

A. R. Ammons and the Poetics of Widening Scope (1994)

Nonfiction:

The Athletic Eye (1984)

Castles in the Sand (1982)

ACKNOWLEDGEMENTS

My thanks to the editors of the following journals where these poems first appeared:

Abalone Moon: "Goddess of Watermelons," "About Love," "Viento Libre."

Alabama Literary Review: "Beachside," "Tropicalized."

The Beloit Poetry Journal: "Lao Tzu's Sister's Dream."

Critical Quarterly (England): "Walking the Loop."

The Iowa Source: "Driving Through A Painting by Monet," "White Nut of Desire," originally published as "The Last Freight Car."

Jewish Currents: "When You Leave Jerusalem."

Judaism: "Tolstoy in Palestine."

The Literary Review: "Return."

Midwest Streams and Trails: "Platte River Liftoff," originally published as "Companionship."

Nebraska Poets Calendar, 2002: "Chanukah Lights Tonight."

The Nebraska Review: "February Etude."

Shirim: "Day on the Dead Sea," "Ninth of Av," "My Wife."

Shofar: "The Expectant Father," "Town of Ghosts," "Gad," "Our Exalted Guests."

"Joseph," "Zebulun," "Asher," and "Unexpected Guests" are reprinted from *Prairie Schooner*, by permission of the University of Nebraska Press, copyright 1997 and 2001, the University of Nebraska Press. "Joseph," "Zebulun," and "Asher" were also published in *The Prairie Schooner Anthology of Contemporary Jewish American Writing*, 1998, the University of Nebraska Press. "Chanukah Lights Tonight" was selected by Ted Kooser for the *American Life in Poetry* website and column. This weekly column is supported by The Poetry Foundation, The Library of Congress, and the Department of English at the University of Nebraska-Lincoln. "Postponing the Start of Another Day" appeared in the anthology *Eclipsed Moon Coins: Twenty-Six Visionary Poets*, published by Blue Light Press. "Walking Beside Calamus Reservoir" and "Prairie Air Show" were first published in *A Prairie Mosaic: An Atlas of Central Nebraska's Land, Culture, and Nature* by the University of Nebraska at Kearney.

The following poems appeared in the chapbook *Prairie Air Show* (Hurakan Press, College of the Mainland, 2000). "Thinking of Frank O'Hara on the Tom Osborne Highway in Hastings, Nebraska," "Spring Storms," "Walking Beside Calamus Reservoir," "Prairie Air Show," "Prayer/Bird Song," "Platte River Liftoff," "Chanukah Lights Tonight," and "February Etude." Copyright belongs to author.

I want to thank the following for their helpful advice on many of these poems: Thomas Centolella, Louis Simpson, Reefka Schneider, Diane Frank, and Daniel Tobin.

TABLE OF CONTENTS

III. When You Leave Jerusalem

Notes 74

About the Author 76

I.

ABOUT LOVE

February Etude

You went out and bought *The Essence of Miles Davis*
this weekend in mid-February
when the sun finally said "peek-a-boo,"
the snow melting into rivulets down the driveway.
You thought Miles might help you with some interior melting,
after the tightness of winter
here in the Platte River Valley
where the rivers are locked with ice,
the only movement on the landscape
Canada geese flying somewhere
but you don't know where
so you turn on Miles, something familiar
& listen to "Someday My Prince Will Come,"
which could mean love
but also something like self-knowledge.
You sit back on your futon
close your eyes
& think
in another few weeks the cranes will be here,
the big birds that bunch together on the river,
spending their daylight hours
pilfering the neighbors' corn fields.
But that's the future, man.
The music is now.
Miles is playing his horn!
You need to listen to him
if the Prince is to come
so that you can feel the melting of the snow
& let go
of that which has chilled your heart
this winter
in Nebraska.

If the Prince is the sun
shining in your backyard
on a Sunday in February
he is warming the earth
                    for the gladiolas
                              of spring.
Listen, the Prince is blowing his horn.

LOVE UNDERGROUND

We live in a basement apartment,
like two hobbits underground.
Sometimes, in the middle of the night,
you roll over. Then I roll over.
And our ankles touch,
and intertwine like ivy
on walls back East.

Sometimes, in the middle of the night,
you wheeze
and I breathe hoarsely
and our hole in the ground
swells with molecules of desire —
for wide verandahs with sunlight,
a view of the ocean and its breeze.

Sometimes, in the middle of the night
we sleep through it.
We do not touch.
We hardly breathe.
We do not dream.
On nights like these
who could mind
living underground?

And, in the morning,
when we walk outside,
who could mind
when we bend to blooming purple irises
our landlady has planted
in the beds
above our windows?

THE EXPECTANT FATHER

You are living through a period of extreme "self-awareness,"
about birth, about death.
Would you feel better
if you were more like a woman?
Would you be less anxious
if you were a sea horse?
Of course, you are concerned about money.
Tell them the male obstetrician means nothing to you.
Tell them you feel no rivalry with the fetus.
Do you engage in "super-masculine" activities?
Play matador to the living room chairs?
You are the bull now,
the king who has
launched the seed
of a thousand collisions
of order.
Shammai says — two sons to be a man.
Hillel — one son and one daughter.
"Male and female He created them."
For you,
bonding with this first unborn baby
is challenge enough.
When you press your ear to your wife's belly
you hear more than the sound of the sea —
the "swoosh, swoosh, boom, boom"
heartfelt precision —
waves of love or destiny.

You have a right to be proud,
but don't be.
You have a right to be foolish,
but be careful.
You have a right to be passionate,
but not if you're on top.
Remember, if you feel ambivalent
about your changing body
take a tip from the Yemenites —
hang a "hamsikah" about your neck
for an easy pregnancy.

Thinking of Frank O'Hara on the Tom Osborne Highway in Hastings, Nebraska

It's Black Friday though the sun was out all day
in Platte River Valley territory
and we had a 10 pound turkey yesterday
with Stan and Marguerite and spouses
the kids didn't act up too badly
and today we took a ride down to Hastings
along Tom Osborne Highway
the geese were out overhead
it was up into the sixties for the Huskers game
so there must be something to global warming
because we could remember Thanksgivings in Iowa
when the wind chill was minus eight degrees
and blew the snow into drifts as high as our windows
but today the sun was out all day
it was so balmy
my wife kept talking on the ride about moving to Hawaii
it's only an option baby like the geese overhead
considering the vectors of flight
and I think of Frank O'Hara
on our way back from Champions in Hastings
with its indoor water slides
how O'Hara knew life was nothing more
than a water slide of experience
so that when he walked around at lunchtime
carrying two good luck pieces in his pocket
he worked these into his poem as naturally
as the construction workers on the city streets of Manhattan

that's why I give you Ganesh and Mahalakshmi
who arrived today in the mailbox on a card from Yossi
adorned in silken robes and flowers
Mahalakshmi wearing a gold ring in her nose
bedecked in a crown of jewels
I wonder if she will bring us fortune
while Ganesh is holding in his hands the keys to a better future
the long tusk of experience before us like the divine path
the geese must know in the fly zone above our heads

POSTPONING THE START OF ANOTHER DAY

It's 4 a.m. and the baby is between sleep cycles.
It's the time when the "little man" who rents space
inside the heating vents starts knocking,
and my son starts crying,
inevitable as fall.
I tiptoe into the room as if something can still be done —
saying "shh, shh" to no one in particular,
hoping that at least one of them will listen.
But the "little man" is hell-bent on knocking.
He's got something against sleep,
against fathers.
I am trying to delay the start of another day.
My little boy rolls over and coughs.
We could get up and do all sorts of things;
the trucks are in the living room,
parked inside a heated garage:
the blue truck with the silver eagle,
the red truck with its flashy decals —
and the brown box he jumps inside of like a cat.

I lie down on a mattress beside the crib.
We are both on our backs now, breathing easier,
and just as we float into dream
the "little man" inside the vents begins scheming,
rubbing his hands, clicking his teeth and knuckles,
banging his knees together louder than any cricket —
"tap, tap, tap, da, da, da."
This is no baby's talk.
It is worse than the ten plagues,
more intolerable than the loss of summer,
harder to bear than inflated intestines.

I try to keep a low profile.
Avoid alcohol.
Don't smoke.
Eat lightly.
Yet the "little man" is wearing me out.

I try to reason with him.
Listen, don't you know God separated
darkness from light, night from day.
This is the Divine Plan.
Read Genesis.
Ask anybody.

Suddenly he stops.
The clicking and the clacking cease.
I guess he's religious or something.
My angel, my brown-haired
brown-eyed bundle of nerves and delight
is back asleep.
But fathers are restless in the night.
Freight trains carrying coal and corn
rumble through the dark air
to destinations distant and unknown.
They are impervious to darkness, to light.

A SERIOUS MUSICIAN

for Roni

He sits in a half-lotus,
Erect,
One foot resting upon the ankle of the other.

A tambourine in his left hand,
He raises his right hand in the air,
Poised to play.

Serious,
His eyes are focused and looking at you,
His mother,

Who years later will draw
In charcoal
This portrait of her son.

In his composure,
This childlike Buddha,
Tambourine in hand

Looks confident
As if he knows
The audience will adore his playing.

In time
He will look at this drawing
And understand

The composure of the artist —
Her attention to detail,
The composition of his life.

PLATTE RIVER LIFTOFF

My son and I watch
the sandhill cranes lift off the Platte River
on a chilly Nebraska morning.
One island after another, beating their wings,
making the crane call from deep
within
their long throats,
the sound that calls us back a million years.
We have taken so many treks together,
listening to the roar the melting glaciers make,
the winds in the firs,
and now this, by the river, hand in hand
we see them fill the sky:
a sea of locusts, a tornado, a blizzard of cranes.

Moments after liftoff, the cranes fly east and west,
in two directions simultaneously
crisscrossing the morning sky
getting lighter,
the sun peeling away the lavender cloud cover.
The cranes land in the cornfields next to the river.
Their music moves from one end of the field to another,
and deep within us the joy cells
of the body
light up just like the pink on the horizon.
The cranes bend their long necks to the ground,
digging their beaks into the dirt
between and beneath the brown stubble of last year's corn,
sifting through the matted hay-like stalks,
digging for the bones of mammoth elephants
who roamed this area thousands of years ago.
We soak up the natural music of the scene,
composing in our heads the geometry of flight,
their takeoff and landing on the river.

Chanukah Lights Tonight

Our annual prairie Chanukah party —
latkes, kugel, cherry blintzes.
Friends arrive from nearby towns
and dance the twist to "Chanukah Lights Tonight,"
spin like a dreidel to a klezmer hit.

The candles flicker in the window.
Outside, ponderosa pines are tied in red bows.
If you squint,
the neighbors' Christmas lights
look like the Omaha skyline.

The smell of oil is in the air.
We drift off to childhood
where we spent our gelt
on baseball cards and matinees,
cream sodas and potato knishes.

No delis in our neighborhood.
Only the wind howling over the crushed corn stalks.
Inside, we try to sweep the darkness out,
waiting for the Messiah to knock
wanting to know if he can join the party.

UNEXPECTED GUESTS

Dressed in black coats, black hats,
wearing prayer fringes outside their trousers,
they arrive on our front step
on a rainy Sunday afternoon.

They are here,
in the middle of Nebraska,
where the cow manure wafts in from the fields
these humid days,

and grown men play softball
in the park under lights,
long into summer evenings.
They came to see us from another planet,

all the way from Crown Heights:
their car trunk loaded with books
that read from right to left in strange, squiggly letters;
phylacteries, and door hangings, exotic as moon rocks.

Unexpected, shall we say, and uninvited.
And what could we offer them
if not a cup of tea,
a piece of fruit?

We talk for awhile of the Baal Shem Tov,
and Rabbi Nachman of Bratzlav,
who said "each person is destined from on high
to be in a particular place at a given time.

At that place there is something one must correct."
But what, we wondered, were they here to correct?
Or what was it we had come here to correct?
We pondered only briefly these questions,

dizzying and beyond our reach.
We chatted about the holidays,
about community, about the prairies
and the space between towns.

"Shalom," I said, when it was time
for them to go. Peace. Good-bye.
I walked them to their car
and wondered if they would return again,

where they would spend the night,
in what motel beside some country road,
meadowlarks on the fence post across the way.
Perhaps they will sip tea there to pass the evening,

planning tomorrow's visit to some rancher,
praying, of course, after sunset
and dreaming of a ladder
that climbs all the way to heaven.

About Love

When you come to understand that your life
Is a chrysalis hanging by a thread —
You need to be ready to split open.
You need to be willing to let the butterfly out.

TALL

for Aaron

Tall in that Texas hat.
Tall like a cedar in Lebanon.
Tall like the royal palm.
Tall.
Tall glass of water.
Tall, dark, and handsome.
Tall in those big feet.
Walking Tall.
Talking Tall.
Tall!

AT THE ROADSIDE FRUIT STAND

Here I am at the roadside fruit stand once again.
I can't seem to get enough of ruby red grapefruits,
Valencias and navels stacked into white canisters on the table.
The bright yellow and orange color of their skins makes me happy.
Let me be taken by the contour of their curvature.
I pick up an orange and it feels good, like a baseball in my hand.
I want to throw it as far as the mockingbird flies.
I want to juggle two oranges in the air.
I want to say "gracias" for palm trees and sunshine in February.
This is a thousand miles from the icy Platte River.

I like to hear the give and take in Spanish between the young boy
Selling these fruits and the brown skinned woman buying them.
She has him cut open a valencia on the table.
Its juices sparkle in the sunshine.
She takes one half in her mouth and sucks it.
The navels, she says, are sweeter.
She has the boy empty six boxes of navels into bags.
These she will drive to her nephews and nieces in Laredo.
She is laughing at the thought of her young sobrinos
Ripping open the skins of these fruits,
Sinking their teeth into them like a pack of hungry coyotes.
In my mind I see her driving along the Military Highway
From Mission to Laredo, smiling, the bags of oranges
Sitting in the back of her Windstar.
She is listening to Tejano music the entire way.
The Border Patrol will not stop her.
The bright oranges in the back of the Windstar radiate warmth.

The way that bright colors work in our hearts is a mystery.
I think of the bright orange petals in the watercolor in my study
That my wife painted before her accident.
They are swimming in a sea of blue,
A slight tint of yellow at the center of the outspread orange petals.
This must be the sun of our love.
After the long months of her pain
I want to share with her a basket of these fruit
In hope that they bring her joy.

DECONSTRUCTION

Sitting alone now at the desk in your deserted studio,
I wonder what you were thinking
When you painted this image of me:
This watercolor of a tight-lipped serious scholar,
Sagging circles beneath blue eyes
Peering out through the lenses of loneliness and betrayal.

I cannot sit still for very long here.
I walk out the sliding glass doors
Of your studio
Into the twilight of a sultry, late-summer evening.
In the yard the palms of midlife
Stir in the storm winds blown in from the Gulf.

You have escaped to the sparse prairie of your longing
Far from the Rio Grande Valley.

When I walk back into your studio,
The torpor of your final days here
Settles over the drawing table and unframed canvases.
In a flash I see you were painting
The portrait of your leaving,
The dark blues and sallow browns
Of my despair.

PASEO DE CHACHALACAS SESTINA
For Reefka

On our walk down the path through sabal palms
Willow, mesquite, and huisache trees
Past the green jays and buff-bellied hummingbirds
And the orange sulphurs with delicate wings
In the woods we saw chachalacas
Feeding in branches along the Rio Grande.

We threw stones into the Rio Grande
After learning the names of all the palms
And watched the dark, green tails of chachalacas
Dart in and out through the thickets and trees
Wishing we could escape the heat on wings
That carried overhead anhingas and other birds.

You wanted to draw the Valley's tropical birds
And canoe along the shores of the Rio Grande
Watching the banks for zebra long wings
And the many species of exotic palms
Growing beside willow and huisache trees
Where we could hear the ringing chachalacas.

In the orange groves we saw chachalacas
Roadrunners and several mockingbirds
That first year we rented a house in trees
Like those we saw near the Rio Grande.
Our sons grew tall like the tropical palms
And your need to leave had not yet taken wings.

When the accident threatened the wings
Of your life, the flight of the chachalacas
The majestic grace of the slender palms
All the Valley's hummingbirds
Lost luster like the waters of the Rio Grande
That slid now murkily beside the trees.

We had savored the fruit of the orange trees
And I prayed night and day the fragile wings
Of our love not drown in the waters of the Rio Grande
Where we walked and viewed the chachalacas,
Kiskadees, and the striking green jays
That flew overhead high above the palms.

Now I long for you here by the Rio Grande
With the chachalacas and windswept palms
The wings of birds and the picked over trees.

LONGING
For Reefka

A zebra longwing
Fluttering along the path:
Your returning home.

RECONSTRUCTION

Let us discover that love is capacious
and forgiving,
like the feeling
that returns after an absence —
the coastal breeze at sunset,
the sudden joy of your touch.

Pleasure

The taste of your lips
On my eyelids,
Sweet element of desire,
Then the river rushing
Inside of me.

II.

Loops and Turns

WALKING THE LOOP

1.

You are out walking the loop, a 3 mile circuit
along elderberry, fir and wild blackberry —
water on all sides. Although you have walked this loop
many Sundays, nobody knows your name
or who you are.

It's a question of beginning again,
Of finding that place within
where you can give yourself to what you see,
to what you hear,
where you can say "hello"
and not mind if anyone is listening.

The Western gulls that hover near the shore
have rehearsed the geometry of flight.
They cruise above the lake, dip
when a piece of bread
is tossed into it.

Sometimes you bring your son here.

He is happy to see the boats bobbing
afloat with software engineers, investors, retired teachers —
their caps, visors, and sunglasses
shielding them from the sun
and one another.

2.

For the tightness inside of you to uncoil,
you must learn the secret of walking the loop.
Take this group of Vietnamese refugees,
smiling, talking back and forth
as if their lives depended upon it.

They are happy to be in the park today,
away from some South End side street
with its litter and mangy cats.
They are dressed as if it were a holiday,
their cotton pants ablaze with the color
of pink and orange water lilies.

One of them plans to catch a fish.
He carries his pole in one hand,
his line in the other.
He will stand by the shores of Lake Washington,
far out on one end of the loop
where he can see the city.

He will toss his line out
toward the skyscrapers, the open air markets, and dry cleaners —
out into the lake, and for a moment
forget that he must have this fish
to feed his children.
He will drink in the jagged beauty
of the snow-capped mountains in the distance
and forget
that his wife never returned
from her parents' village.

3.

It used to be every Sunday meant going on an outing together.

Often, the road led to a sandy beach,
or a path through the woods.

But now you are relearning the necessity
of finding your own way.
She spends her Sundays in the garden,
spraying the bugs off raspberries, building mounds of dirt,
pinching the flowers off strawberry plants.

In her straw hat and dungarees,
she is sounding her own depths.

A neighbor tells you he's tried to count
the different kinds of wild flowers
she's planted in the bed beside your driveway.
"More than you see up in the summer mountain meadows," he says.

This space between you now
"is a kind of answered prayer."
Not a cold and stony peace,
but warm, like the evening air in August
out on the loop.

4.

Halfway around, there's a small stone house
that sits close to the shore.
Set back on a wooded hill
is the fish hatchery.

You can hear the sounds of water
trickling over rocks down the stream bed:
a slow, steady stream today.
In cool, dark pools beneath the fir and hemlock
sleek, bright orange salmon
dart among the shadows.
Who knows what dreams they spawn?
And when the fish hatch,
they will make their way into the stream,
down the hillside and out into the lake.

5.

The letter S makes a loop
that if you follow to a logical conclusion
will close.

The fishermen who wait
in the shadows by the shoreline
make a loop of their lines
into which a hook may be hooked.

The Blue Angels in full aerial display
dazzle the viewer with their daredevil antics,
leaving a loop of smoke in the air behind them.

A loop must return, and because it does
you can keep walking
without ever losing your way.

6.

When twilight turns the chittering of the birds to music,
and the ducks out on the lake huddle for evening prayer,
you make your way back.

Beneath a waterside weeping willow,
a group of Cambodians sit cross-legged on the grass,
eating rice and fried fish out of blue bowls.

After dinner, dessert: rhubarb
pie on paper plates.
After that they will fly a kite,
its green and black tail fluttering over the lake.

Their children will curl into their mothers' laps
and dream.
Not an unhappy dream,
but a kind of reverie,
a blending of wind socks and chimes.

One old man will sit apart from the rest,
his teeth missing, and look out onto the lake.
He will be watching for the terns.

If you listen closely,
you will hear the wind moving off shore.
In the distance, bells are sounding,
a kayak glides through the water.
You have been walking the loop,
drawing you out even as it takes you in.

AT 42 YOU CAN LEARN TO BE A LITTLE CRAZY

1.

So you just turned 42. And you *worked* on your birthday.
A ziggurat of bills, memos, phone messages
an unanswered heap on your desk . . .
your in-basket stuffed with warnings of computer viruses . . .
all of it choking you like morning glory.

Birthday. Didn't whisper it to a soul,
though Kathryn, the department secretary who wears a green
silk kimono to work
and knows the names of wild flowers
would have been happy to make you a wish.
You *could* have told your friend, Patrick, the anthropologist.
He still calls Native Americans "Indians."
They trust him.
He would have been happy to buy you a Thai beer.
Or the Hispanic scholar – he at least would have whispered *Olé*.
But no, you kept it to yourself.

So what if you haven't achieved
all that you had hoped.

Who has?

2.

When you drive home to your spouse and children
during what your friend "Cento" calls
"Magic Hour," that time in Seattle
when the clouds lift
and twilight glimmers pink on the horizon,
you spot a new tree in the bed beside the driveway.

Your wife, the gardener,
who has remembered your birthday with a card:
"Oh, my love, come into my garden," —
has planted it.

But it's only mere coincidence, this Asian pear —
Planted on your birthday, an accident
of fate
you seize upon as a gift.
You read into it all the markers of change:
The children conceived but who were never born,
The father who collapsed
shaving one morning in the bathroom,
Your favorite aunt who died mysteriously of lung cancer.
You tell yourself to live like this fruit-bearing tree,
rooted in the soil,
intrepid,
willing to bear the rain, wind, and heat.

3.

It's okay.
At 42 you can learn to be a little crazy.
Write poetry with your left hand.
Climb Mt. Rainier on the night of the summer equinox.
Sit on the cliffs overlooking the Strait of Juan de Fuca
waiting, waiting for a pod of orca whales.
You've made it this far.
You can swim now far across the Sound,
making loops and turns
as you look up at the horizon.

DRIVING THROUGH A PAINTING BY MONET

I love to drive along Lake Washington
listening to Coltrane on the radio
the salted notes of his sax filling up the car.
It doesn't matter if it's evening or dawn or high noon.
I make up titles for the songs —
"Midnight Reverie," "Forever and a Day," "A Twist of Love."

In spring I look out along the lakeside
at the blossoming cherry and apple trees,
out beyond them to my old friend, the water,
blue light of mountains in the distance.
I imagine driving through a painting by Monet,
sounds of the saxophone awash in water lilies.

I don't know what to make of myself.
I can float like an eagle on the notes of the sax,
soaring over the lake toward the daylight moon,
past the fruit trees and the ferny lakeside plants,
past the sailboats and the lovers holding hands,
past the old woman in sneakers out for her walk.

And I can sink deep into melancholy
thinking back on the tragic summer of '68,
remember the women who looked into my eyes wanting love,
King and Kennedy bleeding open,
the music of Coltrane and Pharaoh Sanders
blaring in my ears.

LAO TZU'S SISTER'S DREAM

1.

Shih-Ch'eng Chi was married
and living in the provinces.
One day, though the road was long,
she set out on a visit.

It was spring:
mandarin, cherry, plum —
and she filled her basket
with offerings. So she walked

one hundred stages of the journey,
until her heels blistered.
As the crow needs no inking to stay black,
blisters on a journey are no omen.

In the middle of the night,
late in the season,
Lao-Tzu heard footsteps
on the path to his reed hut.

2.

She stayed with him for days,
rising early each morning
to walk with him by the river.
Surely, you know the river.

One day, tossing a stick
into the water,
ripples dancing on the surface,
she recalled a dream.

"There was an uncarved block
and beside it a piece of raw silk.
My fingers went over them with ease.
I thought of a field, and saw

a plum tree. Leaning against it
a woman gave birth to a child.
She placed him in a wooden cart
led away by two white horses.

The road ran alongside a stream
until they reached the top of a hill.
From there, I could see the water
downstream, passing by boulders and smaller rocks."

3.

Now one story goes, "Old Boy"
or the "Old Fellow" or "The Grand Old Master"
at the end of days,
saddened and disappointed

in the ways of men,
climbed on a water buffalo
and rode westward toward Tibet.
At the Hankao Pass, a gatekeeper

an observer of sorts, thought
"Here's a queer fellow . . ."
and asked him to leave behind
a record of his thoughts.

We all know the book's name,
though I will not name it here.
If you look inside it
there are 5,000 characters

an uncarved block of wood,
a piece of raw silk,
water running everywhere,
round rocks, and down valleys.

CROWNS OF THE SUN

The kitchen of the herbalist
is filled with jars
of skullcap and chamomile.

Outside, in a clear winter night
a crescent moon is tipped on its back,
holding water.

But tonight,
there are no chantings to the moon.
The call is for some other rhythm.

There,
deep inside her earthen pot,
marigolds float in warm milk.

These are the crowns of the sun.
Dandled in the lap of milk,
these are the herbalist's tools.

ONE LIFE AFTER ANOTHER

1.

Doug fries noodles in Bonnie's Deli
and translates Chinese poems by night.
After he serves the last piece of pie,
he lights incense
and hands out bags of myrrh and cinnamon,
then gives us a lecture on the "Song of Songs."

How he works over the flowers in that poem —
"The sweet flag of calamus evokes delicate kissing
of the genitals.
The lily's trumpet shape, the vagina's throat.
The rose stands for seduction."
Then he moves on to fruits . . .
"Figs are lumps in the mouth,
like the kissing of breasts.
To refresh with apples
is an invitation to unfold."

Jerusalem and Ein Gedi,
Gilead and Hermon, Senir and Carmel.
Each a euphemism
for some new position
in the art of love.

2.

Tim is developing a Vedic Observatory
at the end of a soybean field.
He takes me there by car, down a dirt road
beside the soybean plants,
the August sun high above the prairies
in the azure sky.

At the end of the bumpy road, we get out and walk around,
ten structures positioned to create a circle —
a mandala of sorts,
sundials in the making,
bowl-shaped, some with wings
that curve upward toward the sky.

"These are called yantras," he tells me.
"The Supreme Yantra is oriented toward the pole star.
Each yantra functions as a different type of sundial —
one figures the local solar time,
another the rising sign of the sun,
still another the positions of star constellations.
The geometry of nature resets your internal rhythms."

"Not bad," I tell him.
"I could use that, what with the heat and the kids
and my car needing work."

3.

Diane collects past lives like baseball cards.
She shares them with me over dinner.
"I want to go to Kyoto," she says.
"I know I've spent time there, as a monk
or as a pilgrim.
I hear bells for meditation in my dreams.
Just the sound — *Ky-o-to* — takes me back
to when I must have spent hours
in the garden outside the temple,
my eyes closed,
the silence so peaceful I could sit forever."

"But I can't decide," she says, "exactly when that was.
I'm having dreams now about the Holocaust.
In the cattle car I draw a picture in my mind,
the only thing that keeps me from fainting.
I would have wanted to light Shabbes candles there,
in the camps, though I can't imagine how.
Whenever I see smoke rise from a chimney,
my bones collapse into a pile at my feet."

4.

Reb Nachman said: "This whole world is a very narrow bridge,
but the main thing is not to fear at all."

SPRING STORMS

This spring the rain fell each night like swallows
Swooping down and encircling the old barn,
Awakening us from the dreams we follow
On the river, where the sandhill cranes turn
And circle the sky to rehearse and learn
The ritual of return and mating.
Stirred by the strict, sharp lightning that burned,
We walked the farmhouse kitchen and lighting
A lantern, assured ourselves this dueling
In the sky would pass. We stored our wishes
In the silos of our desire, writing
In our journals our losses and riches.
We sat at the kitchen table for awhile
Unhinged from our beds, now free of guile.

WALKING BESIDE CALAMUS RESERVOIR

Walking beside Calamus Reservoir
in September, monarch
butterflies hovering above the sandy beach,
we feel the great lightness
of their wings stirring the air,
deftly as the fans
Willa Cather's neighbors used
on their front porches,
where they dreamed of dusty roads
west and out of town.

PRAIRIE AIR SHOW

Just because
        no one sees

the pods
        of the milkweed

slowly open
        on the prairie

on a cold October night
        doesn't mean

we should ignore
        their white silken treasure

readying itself
        for flight

on a sunny afternoon
        when the cottonwoods

are turning gold.
        Who can say

if the prairie dogs
        sun-bathing

on the hillside
        have come to see

the air show,
        but when a trio

of pods burst open
        and the white silk parachutes

float over the prairie
        meadow

even the sharp green tips
        of the yucca

crane in anticipation.

A Tree in the Wilderness

When I walk outside these fall mornings
I look across the street at the gathering of sparrows
In the neighbor's ash tree, swept of all its leaves.
I hear each morning the sparrows and their common song.
I wonder *if man were a tree in the wilderness*
What birds would land in his branches,
Whether he could live one more day with so much sorrow.
If woman were a tree in the wilderness
Would she be an ash tree or cedar,
A weeping willow or white birch?
The warm breeze of this October morning washes over me.
The pale three-quarter moon hangs still in the sky.
The violins of fall are plucked.
What kind of tree am I, alone in this wilderness?

Prayer: Bird Song

And all the birds utter, each their own song.
This fall morning we hear them near the Platte —
The sharp nasal honk of the upside-down nuthatch,
The higher pitched notes of the tree and song sparrows
Flitting about stalks of sunflowers gone to seed,
The downy woodpecker working furiously at the willow,
Its head darting back and forth in rapid fire,
The screech of the blue jay among the cottonwoods
And the explosive quail flashing over bluestem.
We know the clarion call of the sandhill crane
That roosts on this braided river each spring.
We compose a song out of all these varied voices.
We hold hands to reclaim our tremulous love
Touching the whole notes between us.

WHITE NUT OF DESIRE

I am trying to discover how to slide along
the way one thought follows another
box cars passing on tracks
in front of the produce shipping yard
cantaloupes and crates of cherries
out on the landing dock
the caboose
trailing into the distance
the young almond tree, slender and green in spring
flowers white blossoms
that unfasten quietly one afternoon
white petals on the ground
reminding me of walks by the river
and afterwards
down by the cattails
iced mint tea served in dixie cups
Then one day the flowers disappear
fuzzy green envelopes in their place
that become shells pressed and tanned
in which the white nut of desire grows
and I don't want this to end
because it's asking me to let go
to follow the stream of chaos
through the canopy of mimosa trees
at dawn the night gives itself up
to the sun shimmering on the water
to the grass singing its wetness into the air
my body rises from sleep
releasing its heaviness
and I want to follow this new day
like the last freight car carrying
boxes of San Juan berries down the coast
until the horizon is all that is left

TROPICALIZED

You grow weary of the pastoral elegies to emptiness,
Of crabs burrowing beneath the sand to dig an air hole.

You get up to walk the shoreline
Of the Gulf of Mexico
And look out at the horizon
Where you see Neruda, Paz, and Vallejo coming towards you —
The body and soul of the vast poetry of the sea.

Then you remember the presence of nature
Is not a long forgotten dream
Blown across the Laguna Madre
By gulfside breezes.

You take flight on the wings of a great white egret,
You probe the depths of the sea like a dolphin.

MISSION BUTTERFLY FESTIVAL

The little yellow that flits about
Rivals the carnival's whirl-about.

GODDESS OF WATERMELONS

The goddess of watermelons
Floats in the sky above Ciudad Victoria.
She wears a white silk robe
And looks down on all the fruits of the city.
She floats in from the white stuccoed church
Nestled in the hillside of the Sierra Madre.
She comes to bless the sellers of sandias,
Whose red juices and black seeds run like arroyos
Over hardwood kitchen tables and rose tiled floors.
The soft watery fruit fills the stomachs
Of field workers, nuns, professors of agronomy
Who come to bow at its sweetness.
The goddess of watermelons floats above Ciudad Victoria,
Patron saint of oval green melons.

Viento Libre

The wind is free blowing across the fields
On either side of the road to Ciudad Victoria,
Capital of Tamaulipas:
City of watermelon vendors and outdoor statues of la Virgen,
City of nighttime mariachis, planets, stars,
Civil engineers and street beggars.

In el Club Nocturno,
Tucked in a corner
Of the Sierra Gorda Hotel lobby,
On a corner of the central square of the capital,
A trio is playing tangos and romantic ballads
Late into the night.
We sit at a table drinking shots of tequila —
Cien Años for a long life —
And listen to the drummer, keyboard player, and male vocalist.

The darkness is impenetrable in the mountains
That ring the city.

But here inside el Club Nocturno
The music warms the air like a brightly colored sarape.
A big, muscular woman sits at a table, alone,
Smoking a cigarette.
She looks as if she came to this city
To work in a factory,
Or to mop floors of a government building.
Her hair is gray and tied into a bun
Behind her head.

The darkness is impenetrable in the mountains
That ring the city.

When a patron of the club,
A thin, balding man wearing shades,
Walks up to her table and asks her to dance,
She puts out the cigarette
And takes the floor with him.
Slowly, as they tango across the dance floor,
She is transformed into a hibiscus flower.
The blossoms of her youth burst open
Like sparks blown by the viento libre
Across the sky on diez y seis de Septiembre.

Beachside

The beach bums lounge by the edge of the sea
Drinking beer and watching the girls go by.
What do they know of life's infinities?

The Gulf's waves pound the shore relentlessly
And the breezes blow inland towards the inlet side
While the beach bums lounge by the edge of the sea.

On the waves Laughing gulls glide.
Brown pelicans circle about, plummet, and arise
Inscribing in air life's infinities.

They practice the art of thinking themselves free
Lying in the sun and tanning their hides.
The beach bums lounge by the edge of the sea.

The ocean is a kind of majesty
For those who walk and see the world besides
Themselves reflecting life's infinities.

Is the life of the beach bum for you and me,
Drinking beers and lolling in the tide?
The beach bums lounge by the edge of the sea.
What do they know of life's infinities?

III.

WHEN YOU LEAVE JERUSALEM

DAY ON THE DEAD SEA

The way the air smells near the Dead Sea,
The fragrance of salt in the air,
The sulphur mud packed into carts,
We rub it like children on our skins.
The Hasidic boys from Mea Sharim,
Their brown hairlocks curled below their ears,
Step into the sea. We do too,
After we climbed the snake path that day,
The winding dirt road to Masada's top.
You had worked the land in Esdraelon,
The plain on the way to the sea.

We return to something that has always been there.
We return to prayer that we never knew.
We penetrate the vowels for warmth
And know them as we know each other at night.

Floating on our backs, laughing . . .
No spoonbills, no pelicans, not even a vulture,
Only the salt, the white grains,
And the sky overhead, a blue dish.
We are fragile, though buoyant on our backs,
Weaker than Samson or Jacob.

When we step out of that sizzling bowl,
The heat has relaxed your mouth and cheekbones
So that you look clear, more free, there
By the shore of the sea.
We rub more sulphur on our skins, take snapshots,
Douse ourselves beneath a cold shower

And run for the hot springs.
Your black hair falls from your shoulders.
We slip into the water like porpoises.
We make loops and turns; we belong here.
That night, every letter, every vowel, every inflection
Of that revived tongue we uttered
Sailed to heaven
Leaving behind a trail of blue smoke.

My Wife

She wears silk scarves
and brings me to Jerusalem.

She is a wading bird in the desert,
a date palm flowering in David's court.

She is a pioneer who dances the hora,
dark like women from Yemen.

Her voice is a flute whose notes
climb the Judean hills
and crawl into crevices of rocks,
linking themselves in necklaces
around the fibers of cactus.

My wife is light and brings me nectar.
She is a dove
who opens her wings
and whirls her body over Israel.

TOLSTOY IN PALESTINE

for A.D. Gordon

Like Tolstoy, you longed to connect your life
to the soil.
You turned your back
on property, family, the high culture of Russia —
to live with peasants,
to work the vineyards and orange groves of Rishon Le-Zion.

Your stamina stunned the younger men
and women who worked beside you.
Your labor connected you to the land of your people.
It made you free.

Turning your back on the occupations of the Pale —
Talmudic scholar, money lender,
peddler, victim of pogroms —
You wanted to remake the Jew into a farmer.

Your weapon against history was the hoe —
Your work in the fields a new kind of worship.

With each digging of a row —
you discovered a new rung upon which to climb to heaven.

The sweat bathed your white beard.
Your eyes burned with holy fire.
Tolstoy in Palestine,
you scribbled "Some Observations"
by candlelight in the predawn hours —
"our people," you wrote, "can be rejuvenated
through labor and a life close to nature."

At night, under the moon of Zion,
beside the campfire,
you preached your religion of labor
to all who would listen.
And when the dreamers of Israel
sang and danced,
you joined them
in the hora of the body reborn.

NINTH OF AV

You read to me Lamentations,
and desperately I cry out
we must huddle, close,
like stones in the Western Wall.

Town of Ghosts
for Aharon Appelfeld

The Rebbe's home has become a dairy,
The synagogue a place where people shoot pool.

Mountains overlook the village's mass grave,
The dead haunt the dreams of peasant women.

Aunts and uncles slip by like shadows.
In a town of ghosts, strange things happen.

Hasidim, Yiddishists, Zionists, Assimilationists —
The cart of death carried them all to the grave.

For days you walked through the roads of deep mud
Warming your feet in the lining of your father's coat.

Your mother's pendant shines on an upholstered tray,
Her jewels dance inside the villagers' houses.

You drink the black milk of childhood
Reciting Kaddish for the dead *and* the living.

THIS BLOODY PURIM

Who is this old man
in black coat, black hat,
his gray beard streaked black,
bending down among the debris?

Is he a scavenger
among the dead,
hunting for loose change,
a piece of jewelry,
a watch that may still be ticking?

The blood on the street,
the sound of sirens,
the stretchers with the dead and wounded,
the terror in the eyes of shopkeepers, neighbors
and soldiers who have rushed to the scene,
belie the calmness with which he picks his way
through the wreckage.

Who is this old man?
What is he looking for?

At first, I think he is an archaeologist of the sacred,
looking for torn Bibles, shreds of prayer shawls,
holy words written on stray pieces of paper
that fell out of pockets.

All about him people are shouting, screaming . . .
Yet he goes on looking.
Maybe he's a Talmud teacher from the Yeshiva down the road.
Maybe a survivor
inured at a young age
to pain and grief.
He picks up a hand with a ring on it
and places it into a bag.

Thief! I yell at him.
What do you want with that hand?

But he cannot hear me.
He is looking for body parts — for feet,
for legs blown off,
for severed heads,
for the bones of children
killed by terrorists on Purim.
He wants to return all of these
to the bodies lying in the street.
He wants the dead to be buried whole.
Yet today the body parts are strewn
over Jerusalem and Tel Aviv.

Haman still haunts us all this bloody Purim,
this bloody, bloody Purim.

A Brief Respite

White, cool, indifferent
The full moon rises over the Galilee,
Lighting the fields of both Arab and Jew.

ZEBULUN

Two blue fish swim inside
The red waters of your window.
The letters of your name, Zebulun, hover above.
Their sounds rumble inside the mouth's cove,
Spill out from the palate like bounty
From within the belly of a ship.

Your tribe's members are merchants and sailors,
Buying and selling precious gems,
Shipping oranges and dates from the plains.
To rehearse the distance between ports
You walk the shoreline
Accommodating vision to changes in weather and sky.

Freely, you share your wealth with Issachar.
His eyes hover over squiggly black lines of text
Inside the tent of learning,
While you work the seas.
He breathes in, you breathe out —
Suspended together in the light of this world and the next.

GAD

Gad is the intrepid fighter,
The first into battle
He will pursue his foes.
God shall be the trope of Israel,
But Gad shall be the troop.
His tribe consists of soldiers.

The dark green in your window
Reminds us of the color of khakis
Worn by the army today.
None will be missing.
They will return in safety
Along the same path.

History is the truth that reveals the lie.
In war after war,
Gad's soldiers have not returned home.
The war dead fill the cemeteries
In Haifa and Safed, Jerusalem and Tel Aviv.
And the blood of Rabin still divides the land.

ASHER

Chagall bestows upon you the greatest gifts.
Doves, bouquets, and a menorah
Fill your window with light.
And what is Asher but light —
The inner light of happiness,
The outer light of the body.

Happy is he who dwells in the tribe of Asher.
He will eat black olives, halvah
And rich sweet breads that rise high.
It will be *Shabbat* all week long.
The wings of the dove are flowers,
a twig of peace pursed inside its beak.

The green in your window
Is the tint of olive trees lining your fields.
The menorah is filled with oil.
Happiness wafts like incense in the air —
She pulls the viewer deep and far in
To taste the bliss on her tongue.

JOSEPH

Joseph is a fruitful son. In the late afternoon
In the garden, in summer, the skin
Of the grapes is deep purple. When you bend to pick them,
The neighborhood girls, in their white cotton summer dresses,
Run up to the fence to catch a glimpse of you.
In the heat of the day, they want to burst into flower.

But you never step out of yourself.
You collect your grapes and sit in the shade of a fig tree,
Just out of sight, dreaming of your brothers.
You can see their arrows passing over you.
When Potiphar's wife tried to seduce you,
You did not lift your eyes to look at her.

In the dark, in the cellar of the prison,
You practice your art of interpretation.
The sun's radiant yellow light pierces
The butler's and baker's stories.
You read them as clearly as spring water.
The hard rock of knowledge composes you.

RETURN

The inner voices, the valves of the heart
that open effortlessly
when you enter like a bride
will begin to sing.
There will be no end of song.
And we will visit the Tannaim,
the holy ones inside the gates of heaven.

We will have sprigs of myrtle.
And there will be so much kissing
the moon won't know what has happened . . .
kissing of shawl fringes, doorways, fingertips.
And you will laugh,
and your laugh will reach the hills of Jerusalem,
the valley of roses
and the lilies of the valley.
The fragrance of our love will rise
and you and I will rise
and we will all rise in the moon's pools of light.

OUR EXALTED GUESTS

We enter the sukah and invite the ancient ushpizin.
Our hearts are full like the harvest moon,
A chair in one corner covered with white silk
For these exalted guests.

A vase of day lilies rests on the table.
Overhead the sky is inky blue.
We see the stars
Through the canopy of evergreen boughs.

We were dancers with lighted torches in our hands
Musicians playing the lyre, trumpet, and cymbals
Singing songs and rejoicing
In the "water-drawing" from the pool of Shiloach.

Now we live in a less ecstatic time
Of human bombs and scorched earth.

Still we invite our exalted guests.
Abraham brings with him loving-kindness,
Isaac unshakable equilibrium
And Jacob enters with the cloud of glory.

We were jugglers
Flipping fire torches into the night air
Everywhere the sound of water
As clear and as bright as the stars.

Moses and Aaron, loyal shepherds
Arrive to teach the blueprint of creation.

May our children grow like the fruits of Joseph
Who stands here tall and straight like the palm branch,
Joseph, interpreter of dreams, of the crisscrossing
Of actions and their consequences.

O David, father of the once great and fallen sukah,
Play the notes of your harp in our dwelling!

Still we draw water from the wells of salvation

WHEN YOU LEAVE JERUSALEM

take with you a piece of Jerusalem stone.
Stones hold the city together,
the old walls and the new.
Bar Kochba took with him the angry slab of defiance —
Akiva the solid rock of knowledge.
The painter takes with him the play of light and shadow
on golden stones,
the musician the pebbles of song.
The tourist takes away the stones of ignorance,
unaware of the blood spilled over the shards.
The soldier riding a bus through the Judean hills,
a submachine gun resting between her legs
as naturally as a child
swallows the stones of resentment and fatigue.
In her green khakis
she dreams of other dawns, other nights.
The zealots take with them
the stones of disbelief.
They jumble inside their hearts
in heaps of redemption and fervor.
David slew Goliath with a stone,
an ancient weapon hurled with vengeance
tearing the air.

To build a wall or a house in Jerusalem
is to make a collection of stones.

NOTES

The Expectant Father (page 4) Hillel and Shammai — two great Torah scholars during the period of Herod. *Hamsikah* is a talisman or charm to bring good luck and ward off demons.

Walking the Loop (page 26) Section three borrows with permission from Thomas Centolella's poem "Sun Sang" in his collection *Terra Firma*.

A Tree in the Wilderness (page 45) and *Prayer: Bird Song* (page 46) are inspired by phrases (in italics) from aphorisms in Martin Buber's book *Ten Rungs: Hasidic Sayings*.

Tolstoy in Palestine (page 59) In 1904 at the age of 48, A.D. Gordon, the author of "Some Observations," left his native Russia to live in Palestine. Gordon was influenced by the ideas of Leo Tolstoy and promoted physical labor and agriculture as ways to redeem the Jewish people and the land.

Ninth of Av (page 61) Date in the Hebrew Calendar on which First and Second Temple were destroyed. The mournful day is commemorated by reading the Book of Lamentations in the Bible.

Town of Ghosts (page 62) This poem is based upon an account, by the prize-winning Israeli author Aharon Appelfeld, of his return in 1989 to his native village in Rumania, where his mother was killed by the Nazis. Appelfeld was deported to a concentration camp at the age of eight.

This Bloody Purim (page 63) The holiday of Purim is normally a festive holiday on which the Book of Esther is read. In the story the sinister plot of Haman to destroy the Jews is foiled. On Purim in 1996, terrorist attacks in Tel Aviv and Jerusalem killed a number of children dressed in costume for the holiday.

Zebulun, Gad, Asher, Joseph (pages 66-69) Four poems inspired by Marc Chagall's Jerusalem Windows at the Hadassah Medical Center in Jerusalem.

Return (page 70) Tannaim were teachers of the Mishnah and helped to codify the vast body of Oral Law that became the Talmud.

Our Exalted Guests (page 71) When the Israelites left Egypt at the time of the Exodus, they lived in temporary dwellings, called a sukah, or booth. It is customary to eat one's meals in the sukah during the festival of Sukot and to invite the seven guests, "Ushpizin," mentioned in this poem. Reference is also made to the ancient ceremony of the water libation (simchat beit hashoe'vah), observed during this festival which was accompanied by great rejoicing.

When You Leave Jerusalem (page 73) Bar Kochba led a successful Jewish revolt (123-126 CE) against the Roman occupation of Israel. Akiva refers to Rabbi Akiva, an uneducated shepherd until the age of 40, who became the head of the Sanhedrin in Usha (86-96 CE).

ABOUT THE AUTHOR

Steven P. Schneider currently lives in the Rio Grande Valley of South Texas and is Professor of English and Director of New Programs and Special Projects for the College of Arts and Humanities at the University of Texas-Pan American. He received his M.F.A. in Creative Writing and Ph.D. in English at the University of Iowa. His poems and essays have been published in national and international literary journals, including *Critical Quarterly, Prairie Schooner, Tikkun, Judaism,* and *The Literary Review.* He is the author of several books, including a chapbook of poems *Prairie Air Show* (2000, Hurakan Press), a scholarly book entitled *A.R. Ammons and the Poetics of Widening Scope* (1994, Fairleigh Dickinson University Press), and the editor of *Complexities of Motion: New Essays on A.R. Ammons's Long Poems* (1999, Fairleigh Dickinson University Press). He has won numerous awards for his work and is the co-creator with his artist wife Reefka of the Poetry and Art Exhibit "Borderlines: Drawing Border Lives." For more information about their exhibit, please visit the website www.poetry-art.com.